GIRLS LIKE ME

Katie Sullivan

Contents

Contents

Dear Reader,

Do you ever read about famous people and think, "Wow! They sound so amazing!"? Sometimes it can be hard to relate to people that are famous. They seem so important and special. It is good to remember that these special people were once kids just like you. They played games and had silly nicknames. They learned new things and tried new things. Sometimes they were good at them and sometimes they failed. These famous people sometimes felt scared and nervous. They had to be brave and face their fears just like you do.

Have you ever tried something new and not been very good? Have you ever felt like you were a little different from everyone else? Have you ever known the right thing to do, but it still felt scary? All the girls in the stories you are about to read have felt exactly like you! Even though these women made history, they were once girls who had the same feelings you do.

I'm going to let you in on a secret. You have everything you need to make history, too. It's what's inside you. It's what makes you brave. It's what makes you know when to do the right thing (even when it's scary). It's what makes you a good helper and a kind person. I'll bet you're the kind of kid who will make history, too.

When you read these spectacular stories of girls who made history, remember they were kids just like you. See if you can picture yourself in their stories. I'll bet you'll be able to relate to them better than you think. After all, they were once a kid just like you.

1

Ella Fitzgerald

Ella Fitzgerald loved to sing!
She enjoyed being on the
stage in front of lots of people.
When she was on stage, Ella
felt on top of the world. Ella
was a famous singer. She was
known around the world for her
beautiful singing voice on stage.
Where is your happy place? Do
you like to perform? Maybe you
prefer to play sports or make
art? Finding something you

love to do helps you feel more confident.

When Ella was a little girl, she loved to dance and sing. Her church always had beautiful music, and Ella loved to sing along. Ella would perform dances for her classmates. She loved to entertain them.

Ella's family used to go to the Apollo Theater and watch singers and dancers. Ella loved watching the people on stage! She was hooked. Ella wondered what it would be like to perform in front of so many people.

When Ella was a teenager, she still loved singing and dancing. She decided to enter

a talent show at the Apollo
Theater. Ella planned to dance.
When she got there, the well-
known Edwards sisters danced
right before her. They were
really good, and the crowd loved
them. This made Ella nervous.
She wasn't feeling very confident
about her dancing skills. Have
you ever had that feeling?
Everyone struggles to believe in
themselves at some point. It is
important to remember that you
are special just the way you are.

Ella got up on stage. The
crowd was loud and rowdy.
At the last minute, Ella
changed her plan. She took the
microphone into her hand. She

started singing. Within a few seconds, the whole theater was silent. Everyone was listening to Ella's beautiful voice.

When she got done, the crowd went wild with clapping! They begged her to sing another song. Ella won first prize that night at the talent show. She began to sing at other talent shows, usually winning those, too. Ella realized something. In her normal life, Ella was pretty shy. She didn't like to be the center of attention. But when she got on that stage, something changed. Ella felt powerful. She felt alive! She wanted to sing for the rest of her life.

Ella had the opportunity to sing with a local band. With Ella as their singer, the band got more popular. People packed into theaters and clubs to hear Ella sing. She recorded some of her songs onto albums. Her songs started to be played on the radio. At first, people all over the country liked it. Then the news traveled. Before too long, people all over the world were listening to Ella Fitzgerald!

Ella traveled all over the world singing the music she loved. People loved her, and she won many awards. She just loved music and singing. She loved being on stage. She was glad she took the risk that night at the talent show. She was glad she was brave enough to get up on stage and share her voice. What is something great you can do if you are just brave enough to try?

2

Elizabeth "Lizzie" Murphy

Lizzie Murphy loved to play sports when she was a kid. She could run and swim faster than the other kids. Nobody could keep up with her on ice skates. It was the game of baseball that really won her heart. Lizzie loved to play baseball! However, Lizzie was a girl. The boys didn't want to play baseball with a girl. They told her she was too small.

Has anyone ever told you that you were too big, too small, or maybe just not good enough to play? How did it make you feel? What did you do about it?

Lizzie didn't let it bother her. She wasn't going to take no for an answer. She wanted to play! She convinced the boys that she could help them carry their bats. Lizzie's dad was a semi-professional baseball player. He told his daughter some tips. He let her borrow his glove and balls. Before too long, Lizzie convinced the boys to let her play. Soon she was the best first-base player they had ever seen. There was no stopping

Lizzie! She had found the sport she loved.

When Lizzie was 12 years old, she had to leave school to go work in a mill that made yarn. Lots of kids had to work to help their families in those days. When she wasn't working, Lizzie played baseball. She was so good she was even asked to play on some of the men's teams. These games were just for fun. Before too long, Lizzie started making money playing the game she loved.

Seeing a girl play baseball as well as the men sure did draw a big crowd! Lizzie wore her uniform with her name written across the back with pride. When Lizzie played, more fans came to watch. Lizzie was smart. She knew she was helping the teams make more money. She demanded that she got to be paid, too. The managers agreed. They wanted to keep Lizzie happy.

Most importantly, Lizzie was just a good player. The team manager said no ball was too hard for Lizzie. She was excellent on first base, and she could bat, too. Lizzie never let it bother her that she was the only girl playing. She just loved to play baseball. She became known as the Queen of Baseball. Lizzie was the first woman to play professional baseball. She played as the only woman on teams with men. She was GOOD!

Have you ever been a little different from the players on a team or the kids in your class? How did it make you feel? It can be scary to feel different, but it's important to remember all the things that make you special just the way you are. Lizzie's story teaches us that even though we are different, we can be amazing!

3

Nellie Bly

Nellie Bly didn't just stand around if she thought people were being treated unfairly. Nellie was a girl who took action! Nellie wasn't afraid to speak her mind. She was a good writer, and she used her skills to help many people.

Nellie Bly was named Elizabeth Cochran when she was born. The name Nellie Bly was a nickname she earned

later in life. People remember her as Nellie Bly. She was called Elizabeth when she was a kid.

When Elizabeth was growing up, she had 14 brothers and sisters! She was just a normal kid who liked playing games. Her favorite color was pink. Elizabeth wore pink dresses every day. She liked pink so much that her family sometimes called her "Pink." Do you have a nickname that describes you? Do you like your nickname?

Elizabeth's father died when she was young. As Elizabeth got older, she had to help her family earn money for food. She had trouble finding a job.

Her brothers could find jobs
but because she was a girl,
Elizabeth couldn't make much
money.

When she was sixteen,
Elizabeth read a newspaper
article. It said that women
were only good for cooking and
cleaning the house. This made
Elizabeth mad! Girls can do way
more than that, she thought.
Have you ever read or heard
something that made you mad?
What did you do about it?

Elizabeth took action. She
wrote a letter to the newspaper.
She said that women were
good workers and should be
given more jobs. She was a

good writer. The editor of the newspaper was impressed. He asked Elizabeth to write another article for the newspaper. The readers liked it. The newspaper editor hired Elizabeth to write full-time.

Writers often called themselves another name when they wrote for newspapers. This is called a pen name. A pen name is like a nickname. Elizabeth decided to use the pen name Nellie Bly.

Nellie loved to write. She liked to write articles that made readers think. She wanted to help people with her writing.

A long time ago, if people thought someone was crazy, they were sent to a special hospital. Sometimes these hospitals didn't take very good care of the patients. The rooms were dirty. The food was gross. The nurses were very mean to the patients. No one believed the patients. Nellie decided to do something about it. For ten days, Nellie acted like she was crazy so she could live in the hospital. Nellie was shocked at how people were treated. She went home and wrote a newspaper article. She helped bring changes to the hospital.

She helped make it better for the patients.

Using her writing to make good changes made Nellie happy. During her career, Nellie wrote stories about unsafe workplaces and women not being treated fairly. When Nellie wrote, people listened. She helped make many changes to make people's lives better. Nellie used her writing skills to make a difference.

Nellie's story helps us see that everyone has something important to say. Nellie never believed that girls were less important. She worked hard to help other people see that, too.

Do you have any talents that
can help people? What are some
ways you like to help others?

4

Anne Sullivan

Have you ever had a teacher who really understood you? Have you ever had a teacher who just made learning FUN? Teachers are an important part of our lives.

Anne Sullivan didn't know she was going to be a teacher when she grew up. When Anne was just five years old, she got very sick and went blind. A few years later, Anne's family fell on hard

times. Anne ended up as an orphan. Not many people would help a poor, blind orphan girl. Things seemed pretty hopeless for poor Anne. Then she heard a story about a school for blind children. Anne really wanted to go to that school.

Some people who helped orphans were visiting the place Anne lived. She knew this was her best chance. She had to be brave. Anne told them about the school. She asked them to help her go. The people wanted to help Anne. They got her into the school for the blind. Anne was going to learn so many new things.

Going to a new school can be scary. Anne didn't know any of the other kids. Since she was an orphan, Anne didn't have the nice clothes or school supplies the other kids had. Anne didn't even know how to read or write. The other kids teased her. Some of the teachers were mean. Anne did not give up. She worked hard! Anne learned to read and write. She got surgery for her eyes so she could see. Anne ended up being the smartest person in her class! Have you ever had to work really hard to overcome something?

When Anne finished school, she wasn't sure what she

wanted to do. A teacher at her school had an idea. There was a little girl named Helen Keller who needed help. Helen was deaf and blind. She couldn't see or hear. Anne was asked to be Helen's new teacher!

Helen was seven years old when she met her new teacher, Anne. Anne had studied how to teach a blind and deaf person. Helen was young. She got bored easily and wanted to have fun. Anne quickly changed the way she taught Helen. They did things Helen liked to do. Anne made learning fun for Helen. She taught Helen new words. She would spell words into Helen's hand since Helen couldn't see or hear. With Anne as her new teacher, Helen was so happy!

Anne and Helen changed the way people all over the world taught deaf and blind children. They remained together for many years. They were good friends. A good teacher can have a huge impact on your life. Who is your favorite teacher? Why are they your favorite?

5

Mae Jemison

When she was growing up, Mae Jemison loved to do a lot of different things. She liked to study nature. She liked to look at the stars. Mae really loved to dance. She took ballet, jazz, and modern dance. But the thing Mae loved most was science. Even when she was very young, Mae knew she wanted to be a scientist when she grew up. Do you have special things that

you like to do? Do you have a favorite? It's okay if you don't! It's good to have lots of things that make you happy.

When Mae was little, astronauts were just traveling to space for the very first time. Mae thought this was amazing! She found space and the stars fascinating. There was only one problem. Mae never saw any girl astronauts. This made her pretty mad. She thought girls should get to go into space, too.

When Mae went to college, she had so many things she wanted to study. She wanted to learn more about science. She liked engineering. She wanted to study medicine. She still loved to dance and perform. Mae decided she didn't have to choose. She could study it all. She took lots of classes. Eventually, Mae decided to become a doctor. She liked to help people and make them feel better.

Mae was a doctor who traveled the world helping people. But before too long, the world just didn't seem big enough. Mae was thinking bigger. She was still amazed by space. She wanted to learn more. Mae wanted to become an astronaut. Could a Black

girl become an astronaut? Mae
decided she just had to try.

Mae applied to NASA to
become an astronaut. Two
thousand other people applied,
too. NASA would only accept 15
new students. Mae got in! Mae
was going to be the first Black
female astronaut up in space. It
was a real honor.

Mae studied hard. She used
her love of science and her skills
as a doctor to become the best
astronaut she could. Finally, the
big day came. Mae was going to
go up in a spaceship. Mae was
part of the crew for the Space
Shuttle Endeavor. Mae was in
space for 8 days. She orbited

the earth 127 times. Wow! While
Mae was in space, she worked
on science experiments for
NASA. She helped them learn
more about how things worked
in space.

Mae liked being an astronaut,
but she still wanted to do
other things. She left NASA
and started her own company.
Her company uses science and
technology to help people. She
also became a college professor
so she could help students learn
about science.

Mae's story teaches us that
it's okay to try new things. Mae
had to be brave every time she
tried something new. Sometimes

it is scary to try new things. But it can also be pretty amazing! How have you been brave when trying something new? Is there anything new you want to try after reading Mae's story?

6

Miep Gies

Sometimes it can be really scary to do the right thing. Have you ever had to tell your parents that you broke something valuable? Have you ever had to stand up to a friend who was being mean to another kid? Even when it is the right thing to do, it can still be hard.

Miep Gies was born in Germany. Her family was poor, and Miep was often sick. Miep's

mother decided it was best for Miep to go live with another family in another country. This family could afford better food and medicine for Miep. She loved her mother, but her new family was very kind. She loved them, too. They taught her to believe in herself.

When Miep was old enough, she got a job. She worked for a man named Otto Frank. This was during World War 2. During World War 2, Adolf Hitler and the Nazi party were in control of Germany. The Nazis did not like Jewish people. Jews were treated badly and often killed by the Nazis. Otto and his family were Jewish. Otto had two young daughters, Margot and Anne. Otto wanted to protect his daughters. But how?

Otto asked Miep an important question. He said, "Miep, I want to hide my family in a secret attic to keep them safe. Can you bring us food and medicine?"

Miep said yes. She was very brave. If Miep was caught helping a Jewish family, she could be arrested or even killed. Miep knew helping this family was the right thing to do.

Miep and her husband helped the Frank family. A few of Otto's other workers helped, too. The work was dangerous. They had to be clever. Eight people lived in the secret attic. Eight people eat a lot of food! Miep had to be careful buying food. She didn't want it to look like she was buying too much food. That would make people suspicious. She would only buy what she could fit in one bag. Miep had to shop at different stores.

Every day, Miep would bring food to the family hiding in the attic. She would bring them medicine if they needed it. She would bring them library books to read. For over two years, the people stayed hidden in the attic. They must have been very bored! Otto's youngest daughter,

Anne, wrote in her diary. She wrote about life in the attic. She wrote about being a kid during World War 2.

Bringing food and books may not seem like doing much. But to the people living in the attic, it was everything. Miep and the other helpers kept them alive. They gave them news of the outside world. They were their friends in a very lonely time. Sometimes a small act of kindness can be a big deal.

Sadly, after over two years of hiding from the Nazis, Otto Frank's family and friends were discovered. Nazi soldiers removed them from their hiding place and sent them to work camps. Miep was so sad. She gathered as much money as she could. She tried to bribe the soldiers to release her friends. When it didn't work, Miep went back to the attic. She saved as many of her friends' belongings as she could. She saved Anne's diary. She kept it safe in her desk to return to Anne after the war.

Unfortunately, Anne died during the war. Miep decided to give the diary to Anne's father, Otto. Otto wanted to tell Anne's story. He wanted to share her writing with the world. Otto compiled the diary into a book known as *The Diary of Anne Frank*. This book has been an important book for many years. It tells the story of hope in a sad situation. Thanks to the kindness of people like Miep, Anne's story is still told today. Kindness can be an incredible light in a dark time. It is always a good idea to do the right and kind thing.

7

Amanda Gorman

I can already tell that you are the kind of kid who loves to read stories. After all, you are reading this book! Do you like to write stories, too? It can be fun to write stories. You can make up new characters and adventures.

Amanda Gorman loves to read and write. When she was growing up, her mom didn't let her watch a lot of television. Instead, Amanda stayed busy

reading. She liked poems the best. When she was eight years old, Amanda started writing her own poems. She liked the way writing words made her feel. It made her feel powerful. Her words gave her a voice.

Growing up, Amanda had a hearing disorder. Some noises were so loud that they really hurt her ears. She also had a speech impediment. This meant that she had trouble saying certain words and sounds. The sound of the letter "R" was the hardest. Some kids with a speech problem might just be quiet, but not Amanda. She wanted her voice to be heard!

She would practice talking and singing. She would read stories and poems out loud. Her favorite thing to practice was the songs from the musical, *Hamilton.* Amanda didn't let her challenges stop her. She used them to grow.

Even as Amanda got older, she kept writing poetry. Using words to tell stories made her happy. She liked using her poems to talk about the things on her mind. She liked to write about girls like her. She liked to write about her hopes, dreams, and even the things that bothered her.

When she was in college, Amanda won a big honor. She was picked as the first National Youth Poet Laureate. This award is given to a young person who is a good writer, especially poems. Amanda was proud! She liked that her poems were making a difference.

In 2021, the people working in the White House called Amanda. Would she want to write and read a poem for the new President? Amanda couldn't believe it. She was so excited! She studied other famous speeches, from Dr. Martin Luther King and Abraham Lincoln. She wrote a poem called *The Hill We Climb*. She read the poem at the president's inauguration. The inauguration is like a party to celebrate the new president's first day. Having a poem read at inauguration is a United States tradition. Amanda is the youngest poet to ever read her poem. All her practice reading out loud paid off! Everyone loved Amanda's poem.

It is an awesome thing to love to read and write. You can learn so many new things when you love to read. Even when she had a hard time reading out loud, Amanda practiced. She got better at it. I'll bet you can write some great stories, too. It is fun to share your opinion using your words in a story. Maybe one day you will even get to read one of your stories or poems at a big important event.

8

Ada Lovelace

Have you ever used a computer? I'll bet you have! Most kids these days know how to use a computer to learn things and play games. Computers are helpful and fun. Who came up with the idea of the computer?

Ada Lovelace loved numbers. She loved math and coming up with clever ideas. When she was growing up, Ada's mom

wanted her to have a good education. Ada always had good teachers who challenged her. One day, Ada and her teacher met a man named Charles Babbage. Charles was a very smart inventor who also loved math. He created a machine that added numbers. This was known as the first calculator. Charles called this machine the Difference Engine.

Ada thought the difference engine was exciting. She loved learning about it and asking Charles questions. Charles thought Ada was very clever. They began to work together on inventions. The next machine

Charles was working on was even bigger. He asked Ada to help.

The machine would use numbers to solve very hard math problems. Ada wondered if the machine could do even more. She thought there could be numbers, letters, even music notes. The possibilities seemed endless to Ada.

Ada spoke several different languages. She helped Charles translate notes from another inventor that spoke Italian. While she was writing, Ada added her own notes and ideas. She had so many good ideas! She just had to get them all down on paper. She said the machine could be like a weaving loom. It could weave together numbers and letters to create patterns and codes.

One hundred years later, in 1953, Ada's notes were published. As scientists and engineers read the notes, they were amazed. Was this 17-year-old girl designing the first computer? It seemed as though Ada's ideas were ahead of her time. Her notes seemed to be the ideas for the first computer program.

Ada lived in a time where girls were not considered to be very smart. Yet, she proved them all wrong! The teachers and inventors who worked with Ada thought she was very smart and wise. They thought she had good ideas. They encouraged her to write them down. They encouraged her to keep going. Sadly, Ada died when she was only 36 years old. She never got to see a computer. But she changed the way people thought about girls and math. She showed people that girls could be very good at math. She proved that girls were smart enough to come up with new clever ideas.

Next time you are playing computer games or using a

calculator, think about smart girls like Ada. Don't be afraid to try new things and invent new ideas. You are such a smart person! I know you have all kinds of cool ideas in your head, just waiting to be written down. Believe in yourself!

9

Wilma Rudolph

Have you ever had to overcome something hard? Maybe you wanted to go on a bike ride with friends, but you didn't know how to ride your bike. Or you really want to read this book, but you struggle with the letters and words. Everyone faces things that are hard. The important thing is to never give up.

Wilma Rudolph was really small when she was born. When she was five years old, she got a disease called polio. It made her very sick. Her left leg and foot were very weak. It was hard for Wilma to walk.

Wilma had to wear a brace on her leg. She had to go to the doctor's office every week. She had to have special massages four times a day to help the muscles in her leg. Since she couldn't walk, Wilma couldn't go to school with her friends. She had to stay home and do her work. Wilma really wanted to go to school with her friends.

As Wilma got older, she
worked hard. She did all the
exercises the doctors told her
to do. She practiced walking
without her brace. By the time
she was twelve years old, Wilma
could finally walk without her
brace. When she got to high
school, Wilma wanted to join
the track and basketball teams.
Would she be any good? Would
she be able to keep up with the
other kids?

Yes! Wilma was really good.
One year she scored 803 points
for her basketball team and
set a new school record. Her
basketball coach called her

Skeeter (short for mosquito) because she was so fast.

While she was playing basketball, a college track coach saw Wilma run. Boy, was she fast! He invited her to go to track camp at the college. After that, Wilma loved running track. She started winning track meets. Wilma qualified to run track in the Olympics when she was still in high school. She got to go to Australia to compete in the Olympics. She won a bronze medal. When she got home, she showed her friends her bronze medal. Wilma started making plans. She wanted to compete in the Olympics again in four years. She got to work to make it happen.

Wilma's hard work paid off. She tried out for the Olympics four years later. Wilma set a new world record at her tryout. At the Olympics that summer, Wilma won three gold medals. Wow! She was the first American woman to win three gold medals at a single Olympics. Around the world, Wilma became known as the "fastest woman in history."

When she was so sick she could hardly walk, no one knew that one day Wilma would be running in the Olympics. She worked really hard to get better. She didn't let her sickness hold her back. What can you do to overcome the hard things in your life? What are some areas that you need to put in hard work? Wilma's story shows us that hard work is worth the effort!

10

Taylor Swift

I bet it's hard to think of Taylor Swift as a girl just like you. It's true, though! When Taylor was a little girl, she had many of the same experiences you did. She used both the good and the bad times to help her as she started singing. She used these experiences to become one of the leading singers in the world.

Taylor Swift grew up on a small farm in Pennsylvania. She loved to explore the outdoors. She had a wild imagination and loved to make up stories about princesses and fairy tales. As she got older, she started playing records and singing along. She loved listening to female country singers and hearing the stories they told through their songs. They sounded so powerful, and the stories were so real. Taylor would sing along at the top of her lungs. She LOVED to sing!

As she got older, singing at home wasn't enough. Taylor wanted to perform and sing for other people. She started singing karaoke at a local contest. She sang for a year and a half before she finally won her first karaoke contest.

It wasn't all fun times for Taylor when she was a kid. Sometimes, kids can be mean to each other. Kids who didn't understand her love of singing made fun of Taylor. They teased her. They made fun of her hair for being too frizzy. She was not good at any sports. Taylor felt like she didn't quite fit in. Have you ever felt a little left out for being different? Have other kids ever teased you?

Instead of getting too sad about it, Taylor found a new hobby. She started learning how to play the guitar. She loved being able to come home from school and sing and play guitar. Do you think learning a new skill or hobby could help you be more confident?

Taylor took all the things that made her happy and sad and put them into songs. She wrote thousands of songs. She put them to music with her guitar. Taylor knew she wanted to be a singer. She wanted to be on stage singing and playing music.

During this time, not too many singers wrote their

own songs. This made Taylor special. Do you know who really loved her music? Kids just like you! Kids all over could relate to Taylor's songs. They had experienced those feelings of being hurt or left out. They knew the happiness and sadness she was singing about.

When Taylor started putting out music on the radio, her popularity grew. People loved that she was so real and honest. She never pretended to be someone she wasn't. She was just herself. It is important to stay true to who you are. People love you just the way you are.

That's what makes you so special.

Taylor Swift is now one of the wealthiest and most popular female musicians. It is still important to her to stay true to herself. She still writes her own songs. Her fans can relate to all the emotion she has in her songs. Taylor shows us that it's okay to be a little different. Find your strengths and just be yourself!

11

Margaret Knight

Do you like to tinker and build things? Do you like solving problems by being creative? Maybe you are an inventor! It takes a creative person to come up with clever ideas.

Margaret Knight loved to play and create when she was a little girl. Her mom said that her favorite toys were a block of wood, a drill, and a small knife. She would spend hours

woodworking and making new things. The neighborhood kids all knew who she was. Margaret built the fastest sleds. She made the strongest kites.

When she was only twelve years old, she had to leave school to go work in a cotton mill. Many kids had to work to help their families earn money. The mill was hard work for a young girl. Mills were also dangerous. Margaret saw a terrible accident. The event caused her to go home and start tinkering. Margaret created a device to prevent the accident from happening again. She liked being able to use her creative skills to help people. Have you ever had to come up with a creative way to help someone?

When Margaret was a little older, she got a job working at a paper bag company. Margaret thought the way they made the bags was too slow. She thought the bags were too small. Margaret got to work! She used things she had learned at the mill. She made a better design. Have you ever used a paper bag? I'll bet you have! Maybe you have helped put away groceries. Or maybe you used a paper bag for Valentine's cards at school. Margaret created the design for the bags with a square bottom. She knew you could fit more inside a bag like this.

Margaret invented a machine to help make these bags. The machine was fast. It could make a lot more bags than a person. A man saw Margaret's design. He stole her idea! He got a patent for the machine. A patent states who invented it. Margaret was mad! She had to prove that she was the one who created the machine. The man said a woman was not smart enough to make this machine. Rude! Luckily, Margaret had all her notes and journals. She had her designs and ideas on paper. She was able to prove that she had invented the paper bag machine.

For many years, Margaret kept tinkering. She was happiest with a project to plan and problems to solve. She liked creating ways to make life easier. Margaret invented over 100 different machines. Margaret's story tells us that girls can be amazing inventors.

12

Audrey Faye Hendricks

Do you think kids can help change the world? In big ways and small ways, kids help make the world a better place. They can even influence adults. Kids can help adults want to do the right thing.

Audrey Faye Hendricks grew up in a time known as the Civil Rights Movement. She lived in Alabama. In some places in

the United States, Black people and White people couldn't go to school together. They didn't get to eat at the same restaurants. They didn't sit next to each other on the bus. This was called segregation. Many people were against segregation, but in Alabama it was still popular.

Audrey and her family were Black. They did not like segregation. They wanted to be treated like everyone else. Many other black families felt the same way. Audrey's family was friends with Dr. Martin Luther King. They wanted to help him with his dream.

Audrey's parents were part of the Civil Rights Movement. This was a movement to end segregation. Her parents tried to stand up for what was right. They helped in ways that they could. Her family was involved. Her church was involved. Audrey wanted to be involved, too.

Marches against segregation were illegal. You could get in big trouble. Audrey and a bunch of other kids decided it was worth the risk. They woke up one morning and planned a peaceful march. They sang songs. There were thousands of kids there. The police came and arrested them. Audrey was nine years old, and she got taken to jail. She was the youngest person arrested in the Civil Rights Movement.

While Audrey was in jail, she was not allowed to see her mom or dad. Can you imagine how scary that would be? She didn't have a toothbrush or her favorite stuffed animal to sleep with her. She had to share a bathroom with 20 other girls. Audrey had to be brave. She was still glad she had marched. Even if she was a little scared, she was proud of what she did. She knew it was the right thing to do.

People from other parts of
the country saw the pictures of
all the children marching. They
heard that the children had
been arrested. They heard that
some of the police were mean
to the children. They knew this
was not right. Finally, things
started to change. Laws were
made against segregation. It
would not be fast or easy, but
finally things were changing.

A few years later, Audrey was
one of the first Black students
to attend the White high school
in her town. She was good
at being brave. She was a
leader for change, just like her
parents. Later, Audrey became a

teacher so she could help other students. She continued to work for civil rights. Audrey wanted all people to be treated fairly.

Have you ever had to be brave when doing something that felt scary? Even if we know it is the right thing to do, it can still be scary.

13

Dr. Sylvia Earle

Sylvia grew up on a farm. She loved the outdoors and the fresh, cool air. She would sit by the pond and watch the fish. She liked to draw them in her notebook. When she was twelve years old, her parents did something terrible. They asked her to move! Sylvia's family moved to Florida. Sylvia was not happy. She did not want to leave her farm.

When she got to Florida, she discovered the ocean. She loved studying the fish and sea animals. She wanted to learn more. By the time she was sixteen, Sylvia was diving so she could study the wildlife underwater. She loved it and knew she wanted to spend the rest of her life studying the ocean.

Sylvia went to school to study marine biology. It was hard for a female scientist. She was one of the only girls studying marine biology. But Sylvia kept going. She loved the ocean so much.

Sylvia was chosen to go with an all-male crew to study new

fish and animals in the Indian Ocean. Sylvia was the only girl! It was the trip of a lifetime. Sylvia saw plants and wildlife she had never seen before. She even discovered a new type of plant. It was a big, bright pink plant. Since she was the one to discover it, she got to name it. She named it Humbrella after her friend, Dr. Harold Humm.

When Sylvia got back, she heard about a new project. The Tektite Project would let scientists live underwater for a few weeks. They could study and observe the ocean for weeks instead of just short dives. Sylvia was excited! She wanted to be part of this new crew. Sylvia was not chosen to be part of the first group of aquanauts. But she kept trying. Finally, she got the good news. She was going to lead the first group of all-girl aquanauts to live and study in the ocean.

Sylvia and her crew spent two weeks living underwater. They made many discoveries. Sylvia enjoyed observing the sea and its creatures all day. Seeing the fish and sea animals made her want to protect them. She wanted to make people aware of the dangers of pollution.

Sylvia got to work. She wrote books and newspaper articles.

She gave speeches and taught classes. She wanted to teach people how to care for the ocean. She wanted people to love the ocean and its creatures like she did. Sylvia has helped many people learn about conservation. Conservation is making good choices to take care of the Earth. Sylvia is one of many scientists who help people know how to do this. It is important for people to care for the Earth, the oceans, and all the creatures.

Sylvia's journey was not easy. It was hard to be the only girl when most of the other scientists were boys. She knew she was doing important work. She knew she was just as good as the other scientists, maybe even better! It is important to believe in yourself.

14

Katherine Johnson

Katherine was a whiz at school. She just seemed to have a knack for solving problems with numbers. Her parents and teachers were amazed. At a young age Katherine loved counting. She would count everything! She would push herself to count higher and higher each time.

Katherine was good at all of her subjects but math was her

favorite. She liked that in math there was no confusion. There was a right answer and a wrong answer. Katherine studied hard. By the time she was ten years old, she had finished the seventh grade! Most kids are only in fourth or fifth grade when they are ten.

Katherine got a job as a teacher when she got older. She was a wife and a mother. But her passion for math was still strong. Then Katherine heard about a neat opportunity. Have you ever heard of NASA? They launch spaceships and study space. Back then it was called NACA and they were hiring mathematicians. Katherine got a job that became known as a human computer. Why did they call it that? Because the people doing this job were so smart they were like computers. They had to solve really hard math problems with just a pencil and paper, no calculators!

Katherine had to help solve math problems to help aircraft launch and land safely. Here is where things were even more interesting. Katherine was a Black female. Most of the people she was working with were White men. Katherine didn't let it bother her. She knew she deserved to be there. She was smart. She was excellent at math.

Katherine was the person who did the math calculations to help put the first American in space. She did the math to help astronauts land on the moon. Astronaut John Glenn asked for Katherine before they launched his spaceship. By this point, NASA was using computers to do the math calculations. But John Glenn didn't trust the computers. He trusted Katherine!

Katherine worked for NASA for 33 years. She loved her job and loved using math to help the space program. Katherine is considered a pioneer. She opened the doors for women in NASA. Katherine's story teaches us to follow our dream. Don't let the little details stand in the way of doing what you love to do.

Katherine was a whiz at school. She just seemed to have a knack for solving problems with numbers. Her parents and teachers were amazed. At a young age, Katherine loved counting. She would count everything! She would push herself to count higher and higher each time.

Katherine was good at all of her subjects, but math was her

favorite. She liked that in math there was no confusion. There was a right answer and a wrong answer. Katherine studied hard. By the time she was ten years old, she had finished the seventh grade! Most kids are only in fourth or fifth grade when they are ten.

Katherine got a job as a teacher when she got older. She was a wife and a mother. But her passion for math was still strong. Then Katherine heard about a neat opportunity. Have you ever heard of NASA? They launch spaceships and study space. Back then it was called NACA, and they were hiring mathematicians. Katherine got a job that became known as a human computer. Why did they call it that? Because the people doing this job were so smart they were like computers. They had to solve really hard math problems with just a pencil and paper, no calculators!

Katherine had to help solve math problems to help aircraft launch and land safely. Here is where things were even more interesting. Katherine was a Black female. Most of the people she was working with were White men. Katherine didn't let it bother her. She knew she deserved to be there. She was smart. She was excellent at math.

Katherine was the person who did the math calculations to help put the first American in space. She did the math to help astronauts land on the moon. Astronaut John Glenn asked for Katherine before they launched his spaceship. By this point, NASA was using computers to do the math calculations. But John Glenn didn't trust the computers. He trusted Katherine!

Katherine worked for NASA for 33 years. She loved her job and loved using math to help the space program. Katherine is considered a pioneer. She opened the doors for women in NASA. Katherine's story teaches us to follow our dream. Don't let the little details stand in the way of doing what you love to do.

YOUR REVIEW

What if I told you that just one minute out of your life could bring joy and jubilation to everyone working at a kids book company?

What am I yapping about? I'm talking about leaving this book a review.

I promise you, we take them **VERY seriously**. Don't believe me?

Each time right after someone just like you leaves this book a review, a little siren goes off right here in our office. And when it does we all pump our fists with pure happiness.

A disco ball pops out of the ceiling, flashing lights come on... it's party time!

Roger, our marketing guy, always and I mean always, starts flossing like a crazy person and keeps it up for awhile. He's pretty good at it. (It's a silly dance he does, not cleaning his teeth)

Sarah, our office manager, runs outside and gives everyone up and down the street high fives. She's always out of breath when she comes back but it's worth it!

Our editors work up in the loft and when they hear the review siren, they all jump into the swirly slide and ride down into a giant pit of marshmallows where they roll around and make marshmallow angels. (It's a little weird, but tons of fun)

So reviews are a pretty big deal for us.

It means a lot and helps others just like you who also might enjoy this book, find it too.

You're the best!
From all of us goofballs at Big Dreams Kids Books

Made in the USA
Monee, IL
24 October 2023

45119288R00059